Engineering

Cool Women Who Design

Vicki V. May

Illustrated by
Allison Bruce

GIRLS
IN
SCIENCE

Nomad Press
A division of Nomad Communications
10 9 8 7 6 5 4 3 2 1

This book was manufactured by Marquis Book Printing,
Montmagny Québec, Canada
March 2016, Job #121608
ISBN Softcover: 978-1-61930-345-4
ISBN Hardcover: 978-1-61930-341-6

Illustrations by Allison Bruce
Educational Consultant, Marla Conn

Questions regarding the ordering of this book should be addressed to
Nomad Press
2456 Christian St.
White River Junction, VT 05001
www.nomadpress.net

Printed in Canada.

~ Titles in the **Girls in Science** Series ~

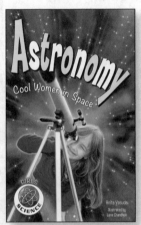

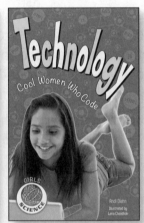

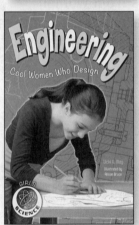

Check out more titles at www.nomadpress.net

How to Use This Book

In this book you'll find a few different ways to explore the topic of women in engineering.

The essential questions in each Ask & Answer box encourage you to think further. You probably won't find the answers to these questions in the text, and sometimes there are no right or wrong answers! Instead, these questions are here to help you think more deeply about what you're reading and how the material connects to your own life.

There's a lot of new vocabulary in this book! Can you figure out a word's meaning from the paragraph? Look in the glossary in the back of the book to find the definitions of words you don't know.

Are you interested in what women have to say about engineering? You'll find quotes from women who are professionals in the engineering field. You can learn a lot by listening to people who have worked hard to succeed!

Primary sources come from people who were eyewitnesses to events. They might write about the event, take pictures, or record the event for radio or video. Why are primary sources important?

Interested in primary sources? Look for this icon.

PS

Use a QR code reader app on your tablet or other device to find online primary sources. You can find a list of URLs on the Resources page. If the QR code doesn't work, try searching the Internet with the Keyword Prompts to find other helpful sources.

CONTENTS

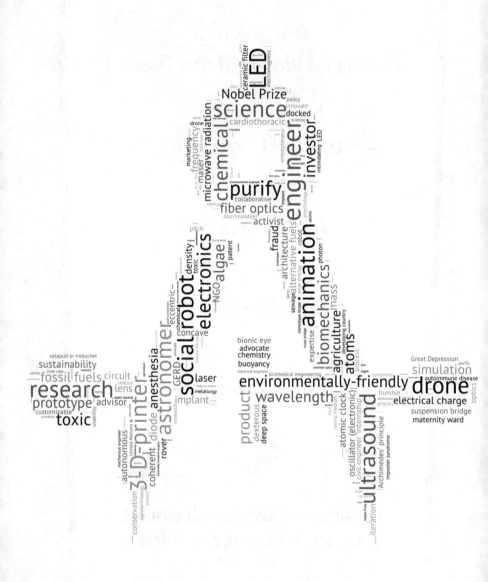

Making the World a Better Place

Engineers design products that we use every day, from smartphones and computers to sports equipment and kitchen appliances. Engineers even design cars and bicycles. Many of the products engineers design help people directly. These include wheelchairs, X-ray equipment, medicines, and artificial arms and legs.

Ask & Answer

What devices do you wish existed? How would these devices make your life easier and the world a better place?

Other products and processes help people indirectly by providing energy, roads, or ways of communicating. Many engineers focus on ways to help people around the world who live in poverty. They create techniques to filter water, provide low-cost lighting, and develop more nutritious foods.

In *Engineering: Cool Women Who Design*, you'll learn about three different women who are engineers. These women have designed devices and processes to help people and make the world a better place.

Amy Kerdok, PhD, is a biomedical engineer who designs medical and surgical devices. Anna Stork is a recent engineering graduate who cofounded a company that designs and markets solar lighting products. Elsa Garmire, PhD, is an engineering professor who has designed and patented many devices that use lasers and light. You'll read about how these women succeed in careers that allow them to be innovative and creative. But first, let's explore the history and the many paths of engineering.

CHAPTER 1

A History of Engineering

Do you ride a bicycle? Do you watch television? Do you use a computer? Do you enjoy amusement parks? Do you have running water in your home? Engineers design all of these products and processes.

While early engineers focused primarily on things such as machines and bridges, engineers today design computers, medical equipment, satellites, and more. Engineers tackle a huge range of problems using a wide range of knowledge. There is something for everyone in engineering!

ANCIENT ENGINEERS

An engineer is someone who uses math, science, and creativity to solve problems or meet human needs. The word *engineer* is based on the Latin words *ingeniare*, which means "to create," and *ingenium*, which means "cleverness." Engineer was used in this way beginning in the 1700s. Prior to that, engineers went by other names—inventors, creators, and master builders.

While the term *engineer* was not used in ancient times, people have been designing and building tools, structures, and weapons for centuries. Many early engineers designed and built roads. They also created bridges, canals, and buildings. These types of engineers are known today as civil engineers.

Examples of ancient structures include the pyramids of Egypt and the Roman aqueducts. Have you seen pictures of the many temples of the ancient Greeks and Incas? These structures were built primarily of stone. Metals such as steel and aluminum had not yet been invented. The designers of these ancient stone structures were often referred to as master builders rather than as engineers or architects.

Designing and building weapons, such as catapults and trebuchets, was also a common occupation in ancient times. Leonardo da Vinci is best known as a painter, but did you know that he also invented many machines and weapons, including a flying machine, an armored car, and a canon?

Try It!

A catapult is a weapon that was used to fling a heavy object. Can you build your own miniature catapult using spoons, popsicle sticks, rubber bands, or other objects found around your home? What will you fling? Here are some ideas.

make easy catapults 🔎

Buoyancy and Density

Why do some objects float while other objects sink? How can a large ship that weighs thousands and thousands of pounds float? It depends on buoyancy and density. Buoyancy is a force that allows an object to float or sink. Density is the mass of something compared to how much space it takes up. Watch these videos to see buoyancy and density at work, and how Archimedes made his famous discovery.

why do things float 🔍   density Archimedes gold crown 🔍

Metallurgy, which is the study of metals, was popular in ancient times. Precious metals such as gold and silver were of particular interest. Maybe you've heard of the Archimedes' principle? Archimedes is said to have determined whether King Heiro II's crown was made with pure gold or not. He did this using principles of buoyancy and density.

One of the first known female engineers lived 1,600 years ago. She was a Greek woman named Hypatia, who lived in Alexandria, Egypt. Hypatia is said to have used the Archimedes' principle to invent or improve the hydrometer, which is a tool for measuring the density of liquids. Different liquids have different densities. Think about honey compared to water. Which do you think is more dense?

> **66** To understand the things that are at our door is the best preparation for understanding those that lie beyond. **99**
>
> —**Hypatia**

ENGINEERS IN THE INDUSTRIAL AGE

The Industrial Age was the period of time beginning in the late 1700s. This is when civilization moved from agriculture to industry. It was a time of many new inventions and machines.

With the Industrial Age came many changes, such as the production of different materials, including iron and steel. Other advancements included running water, machines driven by steam, and mass production. The Industrial Age was also when engineering began to be seen as a profession, driven by the need for more technical expertise.

Ask & Answer

How did early civilizations create technology and systems to meet the needs of community and individuals?

The production of new materials, such as iron and then steel, had a huge impact. Buildings and bridges changed dramatically with the introduction of metals. Prior to the Industrial Age, buildings and bridges were largely built using stone, with no reinforcement. Therefore, bridges were heavy with short spans. Metals allowed bridges to be built that were much lighter and with much greater spans. And buildings could now include large open spaces inside.

The Iron Bridge in Coalbrookdale, England, was the first bridge built using iron, in 1785. It was designed as an arch bridge, reminiscent of the many stone arch bridges in existence at the time. As people got more and more used to metals, the forms evolved to include suspension bridges and truss bridges. These types of bridges were not possible using only stone.

Emily Warren Roebling (1843-1903)

Emily did not have a degree in engineering, but she studied math, materials, and construction methods on her own. She did this to help her husband, Washington Roebling, build the Brooklyn Bridge in New York. The Brooklyn Bridge was designed in 1869 by John A. Roebling, Washington's father. It is one of the oldest suspension bridges in the world.

Iron Bridge

The Iron Bridge in Coalbrookdale, England, was the first bridge built using iron, in 1785.

John A. Roebling died before the construction of the bridge was completed and his son took over. When Washington became ill and was partially paralyzed in 1872, Emily took over the day-to-day construction of the Brooklyn Bridge for her husband. She was considered the chief engineer for the project. Emily was the first to cross the bridge by carriage when it opened in 1883, and she held a rooster during the crossing as a sign of victory.

Try It!

Try building a bridge out of uncooked spaghetti and then try building one out of wood. Which material works better? Why? The difference is similar to building using stone and suddenly having steel as an option.

With the production of iron and steel came other options, such as the ability to make machines. One of the most notable of these was the steam engine. A steam engine uses steam to produce rotational motion. Early steam engines were used to power machines to make yarn and then weave the yarn to create fabric. They were also used to power ships, automobiles, and railways. Imagine how the steam engine changed the way people lived their lives!

66 The world would be a better place if more engineers, like me, hated technology. The stuff I design, if I'm successful, nobody will ever notice. Things will just work and be self-managing. 99

—Radia Perlman,
inventor of TORTIS,
a programming language for children

Several engineering schools started during the Industrial Age, including the École Polytechnique in France and West Point Academy in New York. Women were not admitted to École Polytechnique until 1972 or to West Point Academy until 1976. Other colleges let women attend earlier.

Nora Stanton Blatch Barney was the first woman to receive an engineering degree, from Cornell University in 1905. In addition to working as an engineer and being a mother, she wrote and fought for women's rights and for world peace.

Nora Stanton Blatch Barney
First woman to receive an engineering degree.

Helen Augusta Blanchard
(1840–1922)

One of the greatest inventors of the Industrial Age was Helen Augusta Blanchard. Helen was born in Maine and she held 28 patents. A patent is a set of rights granted to the inventor of a product or process. These rights protect the inventor from other people stealing their idea. Most of Helen's patents were related to sewing. Her first patent was for a zigzag sewing machine in 1873.

ENGINEERS TODAY

Today, the options in engineering are endless. Recent advances in optics, robotics, nanotechnology, and 3-D printing make products and processes possible that were not even imaginable in the past.

Robotics combines many aspects of engineering, including mechanical engineering, electrical engineering, and computer engineering. Even psychology is used to design robots that are capable of performing many tasks. New robot systems that work with the human brain to control motion are even being invented.

Olive Dennis (1885-1957)

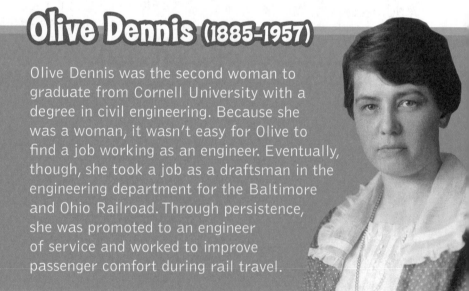

Olive Dennis was the second woman to graduate from Cornell University with a degree in civil engineering. Because she was a woman, it wasn't easy for Olive to find a job working as an engineer. Eventually, though, she took a job as a draftsman in the engineering department for the Baltimore and Ohio Railroad. Through persistence, she was promoted to an engineer of service and worked to improve passenger comfort during rail travel.

Nanotechnology is the study and development of products and processes at a very small scale. One nanometer is a billionth of a meter. How small is that? Here are a couple of examples from the National Nanotechnology Initiative.

- A sheet of newspaper is about 100,000 nanometers thick.

- If a marble were a nanometer, then one meter would be the size of the earth.

Engineers are using nanotechnology to develop new materials to create many things, such as medical devices and computer parts. One exciting application of nanotechnology is creating nanoparticles that fight cancer cells.

Olive invented and patented a ventilator system for trains and helped design many things, including air conditioning, reclining seats, and dimmable lights. She was the first female member of the American Railway Engineering Association.

66 No matter how successful a business may seem to be, it can gain even greater success if it gives consideration to the woman's viewpoint. 99

—Olive Dennis

Have you see a 3-D printer at work? A 3-D printer works much like a standard 2-D printer that you use to print documents but instead of printing a single layer of ink, a 3-D printer prints multiple layers of different materials to create a 3-D object. Engineers use computer software to draw the objects they wish to print. Then they print them out.

Materials that have been used in 3-D printers range from plastics or plasters to metal and even chocolate. While many people are using 3-D printers to print fun toys and other objects, 3-D printers are also being used to create never-before-possible objects. For example, engineers printed a new windpipe for an infant who would have died without it. And engineers are even working on printing human organs made of real tissue.

> 66 By learning to create technology, girls learn to speak up. 99
>
> **—Regina Agyare,**
> founder of Soronko Solutions, a software company

Doctors and other people in the healthcare profession are very hopeful about 3-D printing. They believe it can be used to save lives and improve patients' quality of life.

While there are many specializations within engineering today, all engineers share a common goal. They are designing and building products and processes to tackle problems and meet needs. And engineers often collaborate to tackle problems across different specializations.

Some engineers still design bridges. Others develop medical devices and treatments, while many tackle environmental issues and much more. Some engineers work in offices, while others work outside.

BrainGate

BrainGate is a system that is implanted into the brain of a patient who has lost control of their hand and arm. The system allows users to control the motions of a robotic arm through their thoughts. One patient, Cathy Hutchinson, used BrainGate to control a robotic arm to pick up and drink her morning coffee, something she had not been able to do for 15 years. You can see her achievement and read more about BrainGate here.

Cathy Hutchinson BrainGate video

BrainGate

Engineers can work alone or on teams. Some work on computers, while others build prototypes. There is something for everyone in engineering!

WOMEN IN ENGINEERING

Women have made important contributions in engineering since ancient times, but there are still more men in the field than women. According to the National Science Foundation, the percentage of women graduating with a degree in engineering remains less than 20 percent. Why? How can we encourage more women to study engineering?

Engineer Girl

The Engineer Girl website includes lots more information on engineering. Go there for great articles about engineering, interviews with female engineers, descriptions of different career options, fun facts, and more.

engineer girl

While there are no easy answers, people are tackling the issue in a range of ways. Universities are focusing on role models and collaborative teaching strategies. These have been shown to work well for female students. A better understanding of what engineering is and the options for careers in engineering has been shown to help increase the participation of women.

What words come to mind when you think about engineering? A study by Intel, a technology company, found that one of the most common words associated with engineers is *smart*. Other words commonly associated with engineering include *math*, *science*, and *logical*. While these words all seem like okay words to use, do they really describe the exciting world of engineering?

Engineers design, invent, create, and solve interesting problems. Yes, they use math and science, but they also do much more. Engineers must understand people and be creative and thoughtful in the products and processes they design. While some engineers focus on the technical parts of a design, others will focus on its usability and how it looks and fits into the lives of people.

Cool Career: Imagineer

Walt Disney hires engineers to design amusement rides and animations, to solve problems, to develop management strategies, and more. Engineers who work for Walt Disney are known as imagineers. Their motto is, "Create the never-before-seen."

Ultimately, everyone needs to pursue a career that they find exciting and about which they are passionate. Whether you are passionate about music, architecture, cars, energy, medicine, people, or something else, engineering is likely to have something to offer.

Explore engineering today by reading about the careers of three prominent engineers: Amy Kerdok, Anna Stork, and Elsa Garmire. Each of these women have made great strides in a very rewarding field!

Ask & Answer

What areas of engineering are you most interested in?

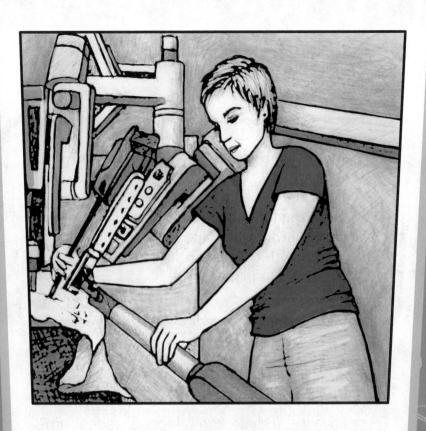

CHAPTER 2
Amy Kerdok

Would you be willing to undergo surgery if the surgeon planned to use a robot? What if it was a robot that you had helped to design and build? That is just what Amy Kerdok did!

Brain-controlled Robotic Arm

Biomedical engineers have developed a way for paralyzed patients to control a robotic arm using their brains. Imagine the challenges associated with developing such a device! Find out more here.

mind moves robotic arm 🔍

Biomedical engineering is a rapidly changing field. There have been many advances in recent years. These advances include surgical robots, robotic arms controlled by human brains, and 3-D-printed living cells. Who knows what the future will bring?

AN ENGINEER FROM THE START

Amy designed and built many things as a child, from wooden cars to Lego spaceships to sculptures, and even a bridge. The bridge was meant to span across a creek in her back yard and give her easier access to her friend's house. She measured the creek, found wood and nails, figured out how to brace and support the bridge, and then built the whole thing in her garage.

After experiencing a moment of pride in her bridge, she realized her fatal mistake—how was she going to get the bridge through the woods and down to the creek? Amy spent a few minutes crying with disappointment. Then she disassembled the whole thing and rode her bike to her friend's house instead.

Amy grew up in Hudson, Massachusetts. Her mother was an artist and her father was a haberdasher, which means he worked with men's clothing. He was also a property owner and all-around handyman.

Like many children, Amy was naturally curious. Early on, she showed an interest in understanding how the body works. Maybe that interest came in part from her interest in sports. As a child she skied, biked, and played soccer, basketball, and softball, among other sports. She was full of energy.

They were a resourceful New England family with a "do-it-yourself" attitude. Her parents even designed and built their own house, which Amy helped with whenever she could. Amy has one older sister, Sarah, an artist who studied English and art in college.

Ask & Answer

What do you do when you realize you've made a mistake?

Amy claims that she and her sister have very different interests. Are engineering and art really that different? Both sisters, one an artist and one an engineer, are designing and creating.

Leonardo da Vinci
(1452–1519)
A celebrated artist and an accomplished engineer.

Little Devices with Big Jobs

The Little Devices lab at Massachusetts Institute of Technology (MIT) designs and develops affordable medical devices and healthcare technologies for people in poor communities around the world. Devices they've developed include the Solarclave, which is a machine that uses solar energy to sterilize medical equipment. Another is the MEDIKit. This customizable device can be used by medical professionals to help with drug delivery and diagnostics, among other things.

OH NO!

When she was eight years old, Amy broke her ankle in a skiing accident. She was told she might never walk again after the accident. She had to have major reconstructive surgery.

While most kids would have found this experience terrifying, Amy was curious and eager to understand everything the doctors were doing to help her. The equipment she used and the exercises she did in physical therapy also got her thinking. She loved seeing all those people learn how to move again in what appeared to be a gymnasium laboratory.

She was by far the youngest person in the physical therapy room. At eight years old, she was strengthening her leg muscles and relearning how to walk. Next to her might be an 80-year-old woman learning how to use a walker after a hip reconstruction, or a 40-year-old man learning how to stretch and sit correctly after having been in a car accident. She realized that everything was connected—your body, how you move, and how you strengthen and stretch your muscles. And all those gadgets are there to help you!

Amy's ankle healed and through hard work she was able to walk (and run) again! Today, she continues to participate in a wide range of sports and also continues to be curious about how the body works.

EDUCATION

In high school, one of Amy's teachers suggested she consider studying engineering since she loved physics, chemistry, and biology. At the time, Amy didn't think or know too much about engineering. It wasn't until later when her mother told her about a presentation she'd heard describing biomedical engineering that Amy started to pay attention. After learning more about biomedical engineering, she decided it was the career for her.

Helen Greiner

Vacuuming is one of those chores that nobody seems to enjoy . . . so why not build a robot to do the vacuuming? That is exactly what Helen Greiner did. She cofounded the company iRobot and helped design Roomba, a small vacuum cleaner that drives itself. Roomba uses sensors to move around your house, changing direction when it encounters obstacles and cleaning as it goes. iRobot has sold millions of Roombas among other devices, including Braava, a floor-mopping robot, and Create, a customizable robot with interchangeable sensors and mechanisms. What chores would you like to have a robot perform?

Helen has moved on from cleaning devices to drones. Drones are robots that fly.

The emerging field of biomedical engineering was a way for Amy to understand the human body. She could look at it from both an engineering and a sports perspective.

When it was time for college, Amy applied to four schools, all of which offered degrees in biomedical engineering. She chose Rensselaer Polytechnic Institute (RPI). In addition to being offered two scholarships to attend RPI, she was recruited to play soccer and basketball there.

As the chief executive officer of CyPhy Works, Helen is developing drones for a range of applications. Drones are becoming more and more popular and are being used in real estate, sports, search and rescue, and more. CyPhy Works has developed two new drones—the PARC (Persistent Aerial Reconnaissance and Communications vehicle system) and the PocketFlyer, a smaller drone. The CyPhy website has a quote that reads, "While we love technology, our work begins and ends with people."

You can learn more about these companies at these websites.

CyPhy Works 🔍

iRobot 🔍

Ask & Answer

Are sports important to you? How do you find a balance between sports and school and other things you love to do?

While at RPI, Amy participated in soccer, basketball, and lacrosse—all while majoring in engineering, minoring in management, and maintaining a grade point average of 3.97 out of 4! This is a very high average and requires an A in just about every class. Amy was also in a sorority called Pi Beta Phi with many of her teammates. She was busy! She claims she did better in school while playing sports because it forced her to maintain a schedule. It helped that her family and friends were very supportive throughout college, as they still are today.

The only B that Amy got at RPI was in engineering design. She didn't let that stop her. She was passionate about the subject and she went on to become an engineering designer.

66 Mankind has made giant steps forward. However, what we know is really very, very little compared to what we still have to know. 99

—Fabiola Gianotti,
Italian physicist

Amy's original plan was to find a job in biomedical engineering after graduating from RPI. But a desire to learn more about engineering led her to graduate school in Cambridge, Massachusetts, instead. She became a Whitaker Fellow and was accepted to the Harvard-MIT Program in Health Sciences and Technology, where she studied the biomechanics of running for her master's thesis. Her mentor was the late Professor Tom McMahon.

Cool Robots

Laura Ray, PhD, and her research group at Dartmouth College are developing Cool Robots that are able to navigate and explore cold environments such as those in Antarctica. Even in the summer, temperatures in Antarctica can be as low as -40 degrees Celsius, so the robots need to be able to operate in very cold temperatures. Batteries and people do not work well in these cold temperatures. Cool Robots rely on solar power and must be able to travel autonomously, or without human contact, over rough terrain. These robots are being used to measure changes in temperature, ice composition, and other environmental factors in cold environments.

Cool Career: Rover Driver

Julie Townsend works for NASA's Jet Propulsion Laboratory in California. She worked on the design, development, launch, and operation of both *Spirit* and *Opportunity*, the rovers designed to explore Mars. A rover is an automated vehicle or robot. While NASA lost contact with *Spirit* in 2010, *Opportunity* remains operational after more than 11 years on Mars. As of 2015, it continues to collect scientific data. Julie is now the rover planner, or rover driver. She is responsible for sending *Opportunity* commands to make it and its robotic arms move.

On June 26, 2014, NASA celebrated the one-Martian-year anniversary of another rover, *Curiosity*. As part of the celebration, NASA planned a special staffing day with 76 out of the 102 operational roles being filled by women.

A synthetic image of NASA's *Opportunity* rover inside Endurance Crater on Mars.

After finishing her master's thesis, Amy decided to continue studying in Professor McMahon's laboratory at Harvard as a doctoral student. She chose this lab because she enjoyed the research and she could design her own program. She also felt surrounded by lots of people from whom she could continue learning.

Through this program, Amy was required to take a year of medical school classes. She also had the opportunity to do a three-month internal medicine rotation at Mount Auburn Hospital in Cambridge. This was an experience that she found to be "humbling and humanizing," she says.

When Professor McMahon passed away unexpectedly in 1999, Amy transferred to the Harvard Biorobotics Lab led by Professor Robert Howe. In this new lab, she studied soft tissue mechanics to help develop models and new approaches to improve surgery through simulation. Simulation is when people practice a maneuver over and over before they have to perform the procedure on a real person.

While in graduate school, Amy also discovered that she loved teaching. She served as a teaching assistant in two courses: "Muscles, Reflexes, and Locomotion" and "Computer-Aided Machine Design." Amy's family is filled with teachers, including her mom, sister, grandmother, cousins, and more, so it is no surprise that teaching is something that she loves doing.

Amy and a fellow graduate student, Sol Diamond, developed a drastically new curriculum for the computer-aided machine design class. The new curriculum required students to take apart a cordless screwdriver and characterize it.

This means they had to figure out the dimensions of the tool, motor specifications, the materials used in the tool, and lots of other details. Then, they used those parts, plus made anything else they needed, to design a remote-controlled car that had to overcome certain obstacles on a pre-made course.

Learning with Catapults

When Amy and Sol taught lessons on material properties for the class on computer-aided machine design, they came up with an idea for Tootsie Roll catapults. To this day, the Tootsie Roll catapult activity seems to be a highlight of the class. You can read an article about the project here. What are the reactions of the students? How does this kind of project inspire learning? Harvard design sweet catapults 🔍

INTUITIVE SURGICAL

After Amy finished her PhD, she took a little bit of time off to mountain bike and travel. Then, it was finally time to give working in the biomedical industry a try. She found a good fit at Intuitive Surgical in Sunnyvale, California, where she has worked since 2007. She started as a clinical development engineer and is now a senior manager in the clinical development engineering department.

At Intuitive Surgical, Amy helps develop new robotic platforms, instruments, and visualization tools for robots used in surgery. Robots act as extensions of the surgeon's hands. They allow the surgeon to be more precise, dexterous, and to see better thanks to excellent 3-D visualization tools.

The role of a clinical development engineer is to translate the surgeons' needs into engineering specifications. Clinical development engineers work closely with the surgeons who use the product, the engineers who build it, and the trainers who teach how to use it.

Ask & Answer

How is a robot different from a human? Will robots ever be able to think? Will they ever be able to have emotions?

Amy's team is responsible for the overall clinical safety and efficacy of everything the company sells. This means they make sure the products are of the best quality possible. Amy and her team need to have a broad range of engineering and medical knowledge!

Amy loves that there is no "typical" day at Intuitive Surgical. She gets to work on a wide range of activities, including talking to and observing surgeons. This helps her to understand how surgeons use robotics in surgery and how their needs might be better met using robotics.

Back at the office, she translates these needs into new products or improvements to existing products.

Cynthia Breazeal

Dr. Cynthia Breazeal and the Personal Robots Group at the Massachusetts Institute of Technology are working on developing social robots, or robots capable of interacting with humans. She is credited with developing Leonardo, a social robot that is able to learn and mimic human expressions. "Robots have been in the deepest oceans, to Mars—but your living room is the final frontier," says Cynthia.

> 66 At first people refuse to believe that a strange new thing can be done, then they begin to hope it can be done, then they see it can be done—then it is done and all the world wonders why it was not done centuries ago. 99
>
> **—Frances Hodgson Burnett,**
> author of *The Secret Garden*

Before new products can be used by surgeons, they need to be tested in the lab, something she also helps with. In addition, she helps teach the surgeons to use the devices built by Intuitive Surgical.

Cynthia and her team have also been developing a personal robot named Jibo that is described as "the world's first social robot for the home." Jibo can take messages, offer reminders, and interact with people in both emotional and educational ways, among other capabilities. Why are social robots useful? Would you want to have a social robot in your home?

You can watch a video about how Jibo works here.

Jibo 🔍

Ask & Answer

Why do new products need to be thoroughly tested in labs before they are used by the general public?

GERD AND DA VINCI

In addition to a broken ankle at age 8, Amy battled with gastroesophageal reflux disease (or GERD) for many, many years. GERD caused her to have trouble keeping food down, which is a major problem for an athlete such as Amy. While medication helped with the symptoms of GERD, she was concerned about the possible long-term effects.

She was desperate for a permanent solution to the problems caused by her congenital hiatal hernia. This is a mechanical problem caused by part of the stomach pushing into the thorax through a hole or a weak spot in the diaphragm. This can cause chest pain and digestive problems.

Shortly after starting at Intuitive Surgical, Amy observed a surgery being done using da Vinci, a robotic device developed by Intuitive Surgical. da Vinci is used by surgeons to reduce the invasiveness of surgery. It improves a surgeon's precision and increases their ability to see what they are doing.

During surgery, doctors have to be able to work inside the patient's body. With da Vinci, they can insert the surgeon-controlled robotic tools through very small openings and work inside the body using a camera to see everything!

After watching da Vinci used during surgery, Amy knew it was time to have surgery to fix her GERD. She wanted her surgeon to use da Vinci, the product she was working to develop and improve. In 2009, Amy underwent surgery with the help of da Vinci. The last thing she did before going under general anesthesia was to check the settings on the robot.

Meet da Vinci

da Vinci is used as a training device and more. You can watch a video and read more about the system at this website. What benefits does the da Vinci system offer patients? Can you think of any dangers? How might engineers solve these dangers?

intuitive surgical da Vinci system 🔍

This isn't typical patient behavior! Amy recovered quickly from the surgery and from GERD and now is the perfect spokeswoman for da Vinci, on which she continues to work. How would you feel about having a robot help perform surgery on you?

DA VINCI XI AND INTEGRATED TABLE MOTION

The product Amy is most proud of is something called "Integrated Table Motion." This is part of the latest version of da Vinci, the da Vinci Xi. It took six years to develop.

One of the main goals for this platform was to make sure that the robot could move with the patient. Minimally invasive surgery, or surgery in which the surgeon does not need to make large incisions in the patient's body, relies heavily on the patient's operating table being able to move into lots of different positions. This includes moving as high as a 45-degree tilt and upside down!

The robot weighs about 1,800 pounds and is docked, or connected, to a patient with tubing. Instruments are placed and manipulated inside the patient's body through this tubing, so the robot and patient must move together.

Stop the Press!

While working on da Vinci Xi, Amy spent time in Europe, where she ran clinical studies on the final product. The trials were quite successful, and the company released the following press release. They needed to get FDA approval on the robot before it could be used in hospitals. How is the language of this press release different from other kinds of writing? What is its purpose?

Intuitive Surgical nasdaq press release 🔍

Amy's team worked closely with both the engineering team and an operating table company to design the da Vinci Xi robot so that it could move with the table, just as people move together in a dance. In that way, the patient can be positioned as needed, instead of fixed in one place. The robot and the tubing move along with the patient and table.

Understanding the human body is Amy's passion. She continues to find working at Intuitive Surgical challenging and interesting. She likes the mix of technical problems, human interactions, and a bit of teaching.

3-D-Printed Body Parts

Professor Jennifer Lewis, a bioengineer at Harvard University, and others are working on developing technology to 3-D-print body parts using live cells as "ink." 3-D printers create three-dimensional objects that are printed layer by layer. Plastic or plaster or metal or even chocolate can be used as printing material. Using live cells as printing material is an exciting new direction. While Jennifer says there is a long way to go before 3-D-printed living organs are available, her research group has developed a custom-made 3-D printer that prints live tissue. They continue to experiment with different approaches. Learn more here.

3-D-printed organs tissue 🔍

One way that you can try 3-D printing right now is with a 3-D doodle pen. The 3-D doodle pen allows you to draw 3-D objects using plastic that is heated up inside the pen. Check it out here.

3-D doodle pen 🔍

What does Amy's future hold? A love of teaching might one day draw her back into academia, but for now she is happy designing and building robotic surgical devices.

AMY'S ROLE MODELS

Catherine Mohr is both an engineer and a doctor. She is also the vice president in charge of strategy at Intuitive Surgical. Amy admires Catherine's ideas and energy as well as her ethical and responsible way of approaching everything. Catherine once told Amy that, "Just because you are good at it, might not mean you like it." Amy took this to mean she needed to find her passion, that idea that makes you want to get out of bed in the morning and brings a smile to your face.

Amy was inspired early on by the story of Emily Warren Roebling completing the Brooklyn Bridge. Emily took over the design and management of its construction from her husband, Washington Roebling.

Emily Warren Roebling

A key player in the design and construction of the Brooklyn Bridge.

Abram Stevens Hewitt, a manufacturer and politician who gave a speech at the opening of the bridge in 1883, said to Emily, that the bridge was "an everlasting monument to the sacrificing devotion of a woman and of her capacity for that higher education from which she has been too long disbarred."

Amy also holds Dr. Franca Melfi, a cardiothoracic surgeon in Italy, in high regard. Franca is one of the only female chiefs of surgery in that country. She stands only about 4 feet 8 inches tall, but she commands a mighty presence. Amy says of Franca that she is fashionable, caring, and humble, and an amazing surgeon, academic, and mentor.

Jane Hill

Professor Jane Hill teaches at the Thayer School of Engineering at Dartmouth College in Hanover, New Hampshire. Her research group is developing devices and analytical tools to detect diseases by analyzing patients' breath. Why would such a device be useful?

Detection of many diseases currently requires either a blood or sputum sample. This is salivary fluids ejected from the lungs, which is then cultured, or grown, in a lab. The method requires patients to wait long periods of time for a diagnosis. For example, tuberculosis is

In addition to her father and grandfather encouraging her to tinker and build, Amy's mother, Gerry, encouraged her to follow whatever made her smile, even if it was unfamiliar. Amy's wife, Corinne, taught her to use the other side of her brain and to accept herself for who she is. And her grandmother, Madeline, who Amy says was a bit eccentric, inspired her to be authentic.

Amy says that she doesn't think it's something special that she is a female engineer. She is just doing what she wants to do. She finds it strange when people think that being a female engineer is unusual. She is just being her.

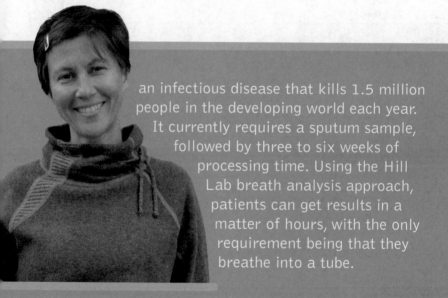

an infectious disease that kills 1.5 million people in the developing world each year. It currently requires a sputum sample, followed by three to six weeks of processing time. Using the Hill Lab breath analysis approach, patients can get results in a matter of hours, with the only requirement being that they breathe into a tube.

CHAPTER 3

Anna Stork

Imagine surviving a major disaster such as an earthquake, tornado, tsunami, fire, or flood. What would you do? What would you need? Human needs are numerous after a major disaster. They include shelter, water, food, clothing, medical supplies, electricity, and more.

The magnitude 7.0 earthquake that occurred in Haiti in 2010 killed more than 200,000 people and injured another 300,000 people. It left 1.5 million people without a home and resulted in a cholera outbreak. The destruction was so bad that, by 2015, Haiti had still not fully recovered from the earthquake.

AN IDEA!

Anna Stork was a graduate student at Columbia University studying architecture when the earthquake in Haiti happened. As a class project, she and her fellow students were asked to design a product to assist with the post-earthquake relief efforts in Haiti.

Many students jumped in and designed new types of shelters and ways to provide clean water. Anna and fellow student Andrea Sreshta first focused on other needs of the Haitian people. Then they learned about the dangers associated with walking in tent cities at night in the dark, especially for women and children. They decided to focus on developing easy ways to provide light.

Anna and Andrea explored many different options for providing light. They tested a number of different lighting products that were on the market. They took them apart and examined what worked and what didn't work with these products. They looked into many different ways of recharging a battery, including solar, crank, and shake flashlights. Their goal was to develop a device that provided light, was portable, waterproof, easy to use, inexpensive, and easy to ship.

Early on, they decided they did not want the device to rely on batteries, because batteries are difficult to find in Haiti and tend to be heavy. They considered candles, flashlights, kerosene lamps, and more, but finally settled on using solar LED lights.

LED stands for "light-emitting diode." A diode is an electronic component. LEDs are very energy efficient, meaning they use less energy than today's more standard types of lights. The LEDs were powered by small solar, or photovoltaic, panels mounted on the outside of the devices. These panels collect energy from the sun.

Ask & Answer

Are you and your family prepared for a natural disaster? Where would you go if you had to leave your home? Where would you live?

Anna and Andrea built more than 50 prototypes of their device by hand. Initial prototypes were built using cardboard, Ziploc bags, tape, and hot glue. As they progressed, their prototypes got more refined, but they learned as much, if not more, from their initial prototypes made with tape and Ziploc bags. The final prototype made for the class project used a rechargeable solar LED light inside a waterproof, inflatable bag. The device was so popular that Anna and Andrea decided to file for a patent and form a company, LuminAID Lab, to market and sell the lights.

LUMINAID LAB

LuminAID Lab was founded in 2011 by Anna and Andrea. While many of their friends were accepting good paying jobs, they were actually losing money in their new business!

Mary Walton (1827-late nineteenth century)

The Industrial Revolution brought many new inventions, including the steam engine, automobile, and other machines. Along with new processes and products came air and noise pollution. Inventor Mary Walton decided to tackle these problems. Mary patented one device to tackle air pollution and another to minimize noise from trains. Mary's air pollution device, invented in 1879, diverted the smoke from factories into water tanks.

While founding a company is exciting, it takes a lot of work and dedication. Both Anna and Andrea believed in their idea and were willing to dedicate a couple of years working to get a successful company started. Initially, they each contributed $7,500 to start the company. This wasn't enough money for a big marketing campaign, so they relied on word of mouth and set up a website.

They needed to raise money to build more prototypes and do some marketing. Early online fundraising was very successful and they met and even passed their goals. Anna traveled to India to test products and get more ideas. They also set up a program called Give Light, Get Light, through which people could purchase one light for themselves and donate another to someone in need. More than 1,000 LuminAID lights were distributed in Haiti through Give Light, Get Light in 2012.

The water was then cleaned up by sewage plants. Frustrated by the noise from trains and trolleys rumbling through her neighborhood in New York, Mary got to work on a second device in 1881. She built a model train set in her basement and made many prototypes to minimize the noise. She eventually patented a device to absorb vibration from the rails. The rights to her invention were purchased by the New York City Metropolitan Railroad.

Currently, LuminAID sells and donates lights for disaster relief and in developing countries, where electricity is not reliable. In addition, they have a version of their product for hikers and campers. LuminAID lights are small (a half inch or less in height when not inflated), which makes them easy to pack for either shipping or carrying in a backpack. Approximately 50 lights fit in the same amount of space as eight flashlights, making them much easier to distribute after a disaster.

LuminAID

You can read more about LuminAID and their products at their website. Do you know of other companies that were founded by people in college? With an adult's permission, do some research online. What do these companies have in common? How are they different from companies that are established by older people? What do the founders of the company learn?

LuminAID 🔍

LuminAID light

They are also waterproof, so they can be used outside in the rain and snow. Because they are inflatable, the light from the LEDs may be diffused over a large area. They are also rechargeable—seven hours in the sun results in 12 to 30 hours of light!

LuminAID works with UN agencies and relief aid organizations, such as ShelterBox and Doctors Without Borders, to distribute lights in times of emergency. After the earthquake in Nepal in April 2015, LuminAID worked with the United Nations Population Fund (UNFPA) to distribute lights to maternity units throughout Kathmandu and the surrounding region. They used the lights to help doctors, nurses, and patients when the hospitals lost electricity.

In addition, UNFPA has established several lighted "Female Friendly Spaces," or tents. These are places where women can come to receive services, counseling, and legal advice, as well as information and support. It is a private space to breastfeed, chat, and relax in friendly company.

> 66 Take successes and failures as they come, since things often change at a moment's notice. 99
>
> **—Juliette Brindak,**
> cofounder and CEO,
> Miss O & Friends LLC

A Long Walk to Water

Many of us take water for granted, but clean water is not available everywhere. Some people walk hours each day to collect water—leaving little time for school or anything else. Read *A Long Walk to Water* by Linda Sue Park, to explore how Nya, a Sudanese girl, walks eight hours each day to collect contaminated water for her family and the true story of how Salva brings water to his village. Nya and her family are fictional characters but the story is based on real families.

A Long Walk to Water 🔍

SAVING THE WORLD

Other engineers are working to find solutions to problems that plague developing countries. Engineers at IDEO have developed the Aquaduct, a bicycle that may be used to transport, filter, and store water. Currently, many people in the developing world walk miles each day to collect water. The water must then be boiled or filtered before it is used.

With the Aquaduct, users collect water in a container in the bicycle. As the rider pedals home, the water is filtered. The Aquaduct solves both the problem of transporting the water and cleaning it.

> 66 Conservation is a cause that has no end. There is no point at which we say, 'Our work is finished.' 99

—Rachel Louise Carson,
conservationist

Build Change is a nonprofit organization that was founded by Elizabeth Hausler Strand in 2004. Build Change helps developing countries design and build low-cost, safe housing. Training is a big part of their mission, and they work with community members to train them on how to design and build safe structures. More than 45,000 homes have been built or repaired by Build Change. They have worked with people in more than 10 countries, including in Haiti, Nepal, and China, to improve housing.

An Italian engineering company called WASP (World's Advanced Saving Project) has built a 40-foot-tall 3-D printer named BigDelta that is able to print low-cost housing! The printer uses water, mud, clay, and other natural materials as "ink" to print the houses. The company is hoping the BigDelta can be used after disasters, when inexpensive housing is often needed quickly.

Ask & Answer

Imagine what it would be like to be without access to clean water or housing. How would your life be different?

Linda Weavers and her research group at Ohio State University are working to find different ways to remove pollutants from water. Rather than using chemicals to clean water, they are using alternatives such as ultrasound, algae, and ceramic filters. Water treatment plants typically use chemicals to purify water, but these systems tend to be slow and environmentally dangerous. Membrane filters are a more environmentally friendly alternative, but they get clogged easily.

Linda's group is using ultrasound to quickly and cheaply unclog and clean the filters. Ultrasound produces bubbles in water that can be used to clean the filters.

Rachel Louise Carson
(1907-1964)

The late Rachel Carson, a writer, ecologist, and nature lover, is known as the "mother of the environmental movement." An ecologist is someone who studies the interactions between plants, animals, and the environment. Rachel wrote several books and papers about the environment and the relationship of humans to nature. The most famous of her books is likely *Silent Spring*. In *Silent Spring*, Rachel advocates against

> **"** Science is not a boy's game, it's not a girl's game. It's everyone's game. It's about where we are and where we're going. **"**
> **—Nichelle Nichols,**
> former NASA ambassador and actress

Ultrasound, which is used in medical imaging devices, is really just sound waves with a very high frequency. Linda and her group are also researching ways to use ultrasound and algae together to remove toxic pollutants from bodies of water.

the use of pesticides. She warns people of the dangers associated with the continued use of harmful pesticides to human health and the natural world. Her arguments are based on scientific evidence.

What Is a Patent?

A patent is protection for a new idea. You know that it is illegal to steal someone's bicycle or money. Did you know that it is also illegal to steal someone's idea once it has been patented? Patents are a legal way to protect your ideas, which are called intellectual property. A patent means no one else can use your idea to build and sell a device without your permission. Early patents by women include the invention of the windshield wiper by Mary Anderson. The invention of Kevlar, a strong but flexible and light material, was also by a woman, named Stephanie Kwolek. A way to fold paper bags was developed by Margaret E. Knight.

AWARDS AND MEDIA ATTENTION

LuminAID Lab has won many awards and gained lots of media attention in the past few years. Back in 2012, when they first launched the company, it won first place in the Social New Venture Challenge run by the University of Chicago. This challenge was designed to encourage students to create businesses focused on helping people. Anna and Andrea used the prize money of $25,000 to get LuminAID off the ground.

Andrea Sreshta and Anna Stork

Displaying their LuminAID products.

In 2012, LuminAID was featured on CNN's *Start Small, Think Big*. The story highlighted LuminAID's mission to have LuminAID lights included in disaster relief packages. CNN contacted Anna and Andrea after hearing about them through the Social New Venture Challenge.

In 2013, LuminAID was named one of the "Top Technology Trends 2013" and featured on *The Today Show*. After the show, LuminAID sold out of all of the lights they had produced!

LuminAID won another prize in 2013, the Early Stage Prize at the Clean Energy Challenge in Chicago. This is a $100,000 prize awarded by Clean Energy Trust. This prize allowed LuminAID to provide several NGOs with more than 20,000 LuminAID Lights. NGO stands for nongovernmental organization. It is an organization that is not run by a government and is not for profit.

Try Building Your Own Prototype!

Are you interested in learning more about solar lighting? You can purchase a kit to build your own solar light or try building a solar oven to roast marshmallows or bake brownies! These websites will help. What else can you do with solar power?

sunbender solar LED jar light 🔍

best solar oven 🔍

NGOs are typically set up to help people and tackle issues such as climate change or affordable housing. For example, ShelterBox is an NGO that provides shelter and other critical needs to people and communities after a natural disaster. ShelterBox has distributed many LuminAID lights.

In 2014, Anna and Andrea hired their first two employees to help with domestic and international sales. They now have four full-time employees as well as several part-time employees. They were also named "Toyota Mothers of Invention" at the Women in the World Summit in New York in 2014. Being a Toyota Mother of Invention "means understanding needs and finding solutions, doing something to make the world as it is more like the world it should be."

> ❝ Can one person change the world? I feel the answer is yes! But they need a lot of help—from their friends. ❞
>
> **—Elizabeth Hausler Strand,**
> founder and CEO of Build Change

All of the women who have been named a Mother of Invention have made the world a bit better. They have done this through innovation and design.

In May 2015, Anna and Andrea pitched LuminAID to potential investors on *Shark Tank*, a television show on ABC. A pitch is a short presentation aimed at convincing someone that you have an idea that could be successful. Thousands of people apply to be on *Shark Tank*, so just being selected to appear is a huge honor. Potential investors, or "sharks," listen to entrepreneurs pitch their businesses or ideas.

Anna says that being on *Shark Tank* was exciting but scary. She and Andrea spent many hours preparing for the show. All of their preparation helped, but Anna still found it very intimidating to stand in front of all of the sharks, with lots of other people watching on TV, and pitch their idea.

Ask & Answer

Are you good at speaking in front of large groups of people? Will this be an important skill to have in your future?

Despite her fears, they did it, and Anna says it was well worth the effort. All five of the sharks offered to invest in LuminAID, so their pitch must have been very convincing!

Anna and Andrea accepted Mark Cuban's investment offer of $200,000 in exchange for 15 percent of the company. He has the option to invest another $300,000 if LuminAID continues to be successful. Even though Mark's offer was not the highest of the sharks' offers money-wise, Anna believed that he had the most to offer their company in terms of advice and support beyond money.

Amy Smith

Amy Smith is a mechanical engineer, inventor, and founder of the D-Lab at MIT. The "D" in D-Lab stands for development, design, and dissemination. Amy's and the D-Lab's mission is to "fight global poverty and improve living standards for developing countries—one low-cost, accessible invention at a time." As a child, Amy spent time living in India surrounded by poverty, an experience that has had a big

Amy Smith
Photo credit: David StellaFoundation

Anna really respects Mark. He came from humble beginnings, but through hard work, dedication, and passion he created multiple successful startups. A startup is new company that is trying to market a new product or process.

Mark's first two successful startups were MicroSolutions and Broadcast.com, each of which Mark eventually sold. He now spends most of his time investing in startups such as LuminAID. He is also the owner of the Dallas Mavericks, Landmark Theatres, and Magnolia Pictures.

PS

impact on her. She sees engineering as a way to help people in the developing world. Amy and her students have been helping people and communities one idea at a time. They work closely with communities to develop low-cost technical solutions, from cookstoves that use corncobs for fuel to off-the-grid energy solutions. Her goal is to help people who live on $2 a day. How can her students understand this level of poverty? She challenges them (and herself) to spend a week living on $2 a day. Do you think you could do this?

Listen to a TED Talk by Amy called "Simple designs to save a life."

Amy Smith
TED Talk 🔍

Mark has pushed Anna and LuminAID to continue to innovate and think about the next steps for their solar light technology. With Mark's help, LuminAID recently launched a new version of their light targeted at hikers and campers—the Pack Line by LuminAID.

While LuminAID has been successful, they have not lost sight of their vision. LuminAID is committed to providing affordable, clean light to people after disasters or in communities without access to electricity. After disasters, LuminAID continues to partner with organizations on the ground to distribute lights through their Give Light, Get Light program. Customers can purchase a light and donate an additional light to the partner.

ANNA'S BACKGROUND

The idea for LuminAID came from a class taken by Anna as a graduate student in architecture at Columbia University, but she was no stranger to design and prototyping. Anna earned her bachelor's degree in engineering from Dartmouth College, where she spent lots of time designing and building. It was at Dartmouth that she first started thinking seriously about combining design with sustainability and social good.

> 66 Focus on constant iteration of your product or service. Never hold too closely to your idea but be open to change and innovation. 99
>
> **—Jean Chong,**
> cofounder and CEO, Starbates

Anna says that in addition to learning about materials, she learned about solar and renewable energy through courses and projects at Dartmouth. Anna was particularly inspired by an environmental engineering course and a materials course that she took at Dartmouth.

She also interned at the U.S. Army Soldier Systems Center in Natick, Massachusetts, while she was at Dartmouth. During this internship, she investigated heating and cooling systems in remote locations and how to improve them.

After graduating from Dartmouth College, Anna headed to Columbia. Anna admits that she decided early on at Columbia that she didn't want to become an architect. She was more interested in becoming an entrepreneur and designer. She doesn't regret going to architecture school because it helped her become more creative and a better designer. And the program at Columbia was supportive of career options beyond a traditional career in architecture. Her background in engineering and in architecture helped her launch LuminAID.

The $300 House

Is it possible to build a house for $300? That is the goal! The $300 House project was started by a business professor at Dartmouth College along with a consultant. The pair wrote an article challenging the world to design a house that could be built for $300. An amazing number of people took on the challenge and engineers and architects around the world continue to try to design and develop affordable housing for the poor.

300 dollar house 🔍

After finishing her master's degree at Columbia, Anna was awarded a Kauffman Global Fellowship in Entrepreneurship. The fellowship is awarded to recent college graduates to help them develop entrepreneurship skills. It helps them to further develop their business ideas. As part of the fellowship, Anna spent four months at Warby Parker, a retail startup.

Anna worked as an operations intern and helped with customer service and order processing. She also shadowed different people within the company to learn about marketing, production, inventory management, and customer service. She has put all of these skills to use at LuminAID Lab.

ANNA AND LUMINAID'S FUTURE

Anna hopes to continue to expand the line of products available through LuminAID. She wants to see more innovative portable energy products for emergency aid and camping. It's about continuing to push the boundaries of designing with solar and integrating different materials and components. She also doesn't want to lose sight of LuminAID's mission—creating energy-efficient devices that help people, even those in the poorest communities.

> 66 These lights have really changed our lives and allowed for opportunities and possibilities that we simply did not have before in this area. 99
>
> **—a teacher at the San Pablo School,**
> Nicaragua

CHAPTER 4
Elsa Garmire

The Great Depression during the 1930s was a time of struggle for many people, including Elsa Garmire's family. Elsa's father spent years trying to find a job that paid well, despite holding a PhD in chemistry. As a result, Elsa's family moved often. They eventually settled in a suburb outside of Chicago, where her father found a job as a chemical engineer.

The fact that Elsa grew up during the Great Depression helps explains why she has spent much of her life looking for and facing challenges. It has been an effort to improve and enrich her life.

SCIENCE AND ENGINEERING: A ROAD TO SUCCESS

Elsa's mother studied music in school. She gave violin lessons, but was mostly a stay-at-home mom. Elsa loved her mother, but wanted more for her own future.

Limor Fried

Limor Fried is an electrical engineer with bachelor's and master's degrees from MIT. She is an advocate for open source hardware and software. Open-source means anyone can use and improve on something. In 2005, Limor founded Adafruit Industries in her dorm room at MIT. She writes on the Adafruit website that her goal is to "create the best place online for learning electronics and making the best designed products for makers of all ages and skill levels."

Limor is the queen of the electronics maker movement and hopes to support makers of all ages. One of her nicknames is LadyAda, as a tribute to Ada Lovelace, a British mathematician known for her work on Charles Babbage's Analytical Machine. This machine is considered to be the first computer. Limor was the first woman to appear on the cover of *Wired* magazine and was named an "Entrepreneur of the Year" in 2012.

She saw science and engineering as the way to succeed in life. She also wanted to figure out how everything worked! In this way, Elsa took after her father, more so than her two sisters, one older and one younger, who both followed in her mother's footsteps. It was Elsa's father who helped guide her toward science and engineering. He thought she had the personality of a scientist and the ability to concentrate and study.

Adafruit Industries is one of the fastest-growing companies and is 100 percent woman owned. Check out Adafruit's supplies to help you get started making your own electronic devices.

Adafruit 🔍

One of Limor's favorite quotes is by inventor Dean Kamen: "We are what we celebrate." Limor goes on to say, "We still have a lot of work to do to get more women celebrated in many tech fields, everyone can help get some amazing women in the spotlight more and more."

You can read an interview with Limor here.

Limor Fried ada initiative 🔍

When she was young, Elsa's father took her to meet one of his female colleagues, who was a fellow engineer. At the time, Elsa's father was working on the design of the chemistry labs for the Argonne National Laboratories. His colleague was working on the designs for the wastewater systems. Elsa was not impressed or inspired by the female engineer, but she was interested enough in what her father was doing to remain excited about science and engineering.

EDUCATION

In high school, Elsa was not good at math. She knew she should work harder to get better at math so she joined the math team. Her math team won a prestigious slide rule contest because they were the fastest at solving complex math problems using a slide rule. The prize was an expensive slide rule that Elsa has kept all these years.

A slide rule was used to solve math problems before calculators were invented.

> ** ""** If this is something that you really want to
> do, if you believe in it . . . simply keep forging
> forward because success will come. **""**
>
> **—Cassandra Sanford,**
> cofounder and CEO, KellyMitchell tech staffing firm

Reading and writing have always been easy for Elsa
and she excelled in these subjects in high school. But
physics was what she loved and what she was interested
in. She saw physics as a way to figure things out.

She recalls that her high school set up a series of
contests and exams in different academic disciplines. It
was a way for students to compete in academics, just
as athletes compete in sports. Elsa signed up to take
almost all of the exams and won many blue ribbons in
science as well as in English and French.

Elsa recently found a pamphlet from high school that
she saved. The pamphlet was an advertisement for a
college that showed different career options for students.
"Researcher" was one of the career options listed—and
Elsa had put a check mark next to that option. She even
knew back then that research was for her.

A white man portrayed the researcher, while the only
woman in the pamphlet was a librarian. Luckily, those
images didn't matter too much to Elsa or influence her
thinking.

When Elsa was looking at colleges, she focused on schools with excellent reputations in science and engineering. At the time, Radcliffe College was one of the hardest schools to get into. It had an excellent reputation. This was one of those challenges that Elsa sought out and tackled.

Radcliffe College was an elite women's liberal arts college and a partner school to the male-only Harvard College. Radcliffe was known for attracting intelligent, curious, and independent-minded students. It was the school for Elsa. At the time, Radcliffe women took joint classes with Harvard men, although they took exams in separate locations.

Helen Keller (1880-1968)

Helen Keller said, "The only thing worse than being blind is having sight but no vision." An illness caused Helen to lose her sight and hearing before she was two years old. Through her own can-do spirit and the help of her family, she learned to communicate, initially using signs that she made up herself and eventually learning to spell out words and read Braille.

Anne Sullivan, who was also visually impaired, became Helen's teacher and companion. With Anne's help, Helen was able to not only learn but to flourish. Once she started learning, her desire to continue learning became intense, and exhausting for Anne. Helen went on to become a political activist, author, and speaker.

Elsa earned a bachelor's degree in physics from Radcliffe College in 1961. Toward the end of her time at Radcliffe, men and women had begun to be more integrated in classes. But Elsa was one of only three women studying physics. She chose physics because there were so many exciting things happening in the field.

After finishing her bachelor's degree, Elsa went on to complete a doctoral degree in physics at MIT. Why MIT? For the challenge, of course!

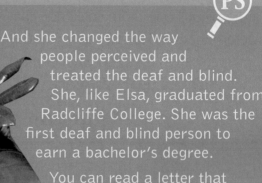

And she changed the way people perceived and treated the deaf and blind. She, like Elsa, graduated from Radcliffe College. She was the first deaf and blind person to earn a bachelor's degree.

You can read a letter that Helen sent to Alexander Graham Bell, the famous inventor. What do you notice about the tone of the letter? Does Helen seem confident or timid?

Helen Keller letter Bell 🔍

> **"**Women shouldn't be afraid to put themselves forward.**"**
>
> **—Sarah Wood,**
> cofounder and COO, Unruly Media video tech firm

Through graduate school and beyond, Elsa's research has focused on lasers and optics. Elsa's advisor and mentor at MIT was Charles H. Townes. Charles won the Nobel Prize in physics in 1964 for his work related to masers. The word *masers* is an acronym for "microwave amplification by stimulated emission of radiation."

Elsa started at MIT with a different advisor, but didn't find the research being done in that lab to be very interesting. So she changed advisors. This wasn't an easy thing for a young female physicist at the time. That's one more challenge that she met with determination. Her advice for students is to advocate for themselves and find what is most interesting to them. For Elsa, that was lasers.

LASERS

Laser stands for "light amplification by stimulated emission of radiation." Lasers are powerful beams of light, powerful enough to cut diamonds and metal. They can travel for miles, send messages through long fibers or threads (known as fiber optics), perform surgery, and more.

How do lasers work? A laser consists of a lasing medium, an energy source, and two mirrors. Lasing mediums are substances with special properties. Gases, liquids, crystals, and other substances may be used as lasing mediums.

Flashes of light or electrical charges are used to "pump" the lasing material to get the atoms in the medium into an excited state. In this excited state, the atoms emit energy in the form of photons. These are small particles of light.

The photons released in a laser have a certain wavelength. Wavelength determines the color of the light produced. The light produced by a laser is a single color and is said to be coherent. This means it is organized, since the photons all have the same wavelength.

Ask & Answer

Do you have any experience with lasers? What do you know about them?

How about the mirrors? What is their role? The photons in a laser reflect off the mirrors, bouncing back and forth through the lasing medium. This excites more atoms, which in turn produces more photons. This is how you can get such strong beams of light using lasers. One of the mirrors contains a small hole to let some of the light through to form a laser beam.

How is a laser different from a flashlight? The light from a flashlight contains light or photons with many different wavelengths. Because of this, the beam of light is broader and more diffuse. It doesn't travel as far.

Valerie L. Thomas

Valerie L. Thomas is an African-American astronomer who worked for NASA until she retired. Even though she was discouraged from studying science and math in her younger years, at college she was able to follow her interests. She graduated with a degree in physics.

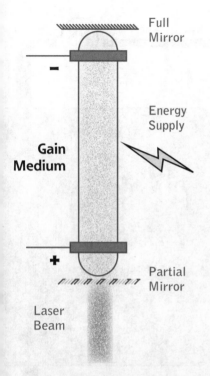

Gain Medium

Full Mirror

Energy Supply

Partial Mirror

Laser Beam

Elsa was interested in optics as well as lasers. The word *optic* comes from an ancient Greek word meaning "appearance" or "look." Optics is the study of the properties and behavior of light. Engineers focus on optics design and build many devices using optics. These include cameras, lenses, telescopes, lasers, communication devices, parts for computers, and CD and DVD players.

At NASA, Valerie worked on many different research efforts, including the study of satellite technologies, Halley's Comet, and the ozone layer. But she is likely best known for her development of an illusion transmitter, for which she holds a patent. The illusion transmitter uses concave mirrors to give the illusion of a real 3-D object projected in front of the mirrors. The illusion transmitter that Valerie invented has been used to help in surgery as well as in the television and film industry.

Optical Illusions

Optical illusions are images that are misleading or might be viewed multiple ways. Optical illusions play visual tricks on our brains so that we perceive things differently.

Try out the famous optical illusions shown here. The first contains multiple faces. Which one do you see? In the second image, are the lines straight or slanted?

Try more optical illusions at this website. Do you think optical illusions can be useful? How?

optics 4 kids illusions 🔎

CHARLES H. TOWNES AND MASERS

The late Professor Charles H. Townes was Elsa's mentor and doctoral research advisor. He was awarded the Nobel Prize in Physics along with Nikolay Basov and Alexander Prokhorov in 1964 for his theoretical work related to lasers and masers. Charles was known as being very curious and optimistic.

Masers were invented before lasers. They produce a beam of microwave radiation rather than a beam of light, as lasers do. Electromagnetic radiation comes in a range of frequencies or wavelengths. These include visible light, microwaves, ultraviolet waves, radio waves, and television waves.

Masers are used in atomic clocks, radio telescopes, and communication devices for deep space. Charles, along with two colleagues, built the first maser at Columbia University, where he was a professor at the time.

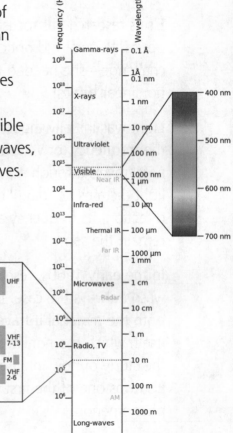

Electromagnetic spectrum

Charles once told Elsa that in physics and in science, it is "most important to be first." His reasoning here was that if you wait to publish your ideas until the research and paper are perfect, someone else might beat you to it. Better to publish and discuss your research instead of keeping it hidden away forever.

ELSA'S RESEARCH

Elsa's research has focused primarily on nonlinear optics. Regular old optics was not enough of a challenge—she needed the added challenge of nonlinear optics!

Light was initially thought to be linear, meaning the frequency, or wavelength, remains unchanged as it travels through materials. The frequency of light dictates its color. So while light might change direction, its frequency and color were thought to remain the same.

In the early 1960s, researchers found that this wasn't always the case. Intense light can change both the material it travels through and the light itself, which is a nonlinear effect. Nonlinear optics is the study of how intense light interacts with matter. Elsa was one of the first researchers to study the phenomenon.

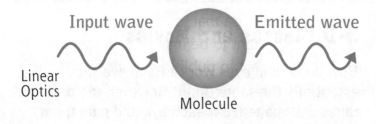

Linear Optics

Input wave   Emitted wave

Molecule

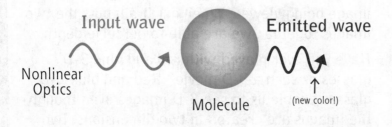

Nonlinear Optics

Input wave   Emitted wave

Molecule   (new color!)

Elsa's early research focused on the nonlinear effects of light in liquids. This was one of the biggest challenges in the field at the time. Nonlinear effects in light can be helpful or harmful, depending on the situation. They are important to understand.

> 66 Nonlinear optics can be many things: good when creating new frequencies, improving lasers, manufacturing, offering new science; bad when damaging optics; ugly in telecommunications by limiting signals through fibers; beautiful when creating solitons. 99
>
> **—Elsa Garmire**

3-D Glasses and Movies

How do human eyes work? Each eye sees essentially the same thing. However, the brain takes the image from each eye and puts them together to form a single image. Each eye has a slightly different perspective or angle on the image being viewed. When our brain puts the two images together, we are able to perceive depth.

Have you ever played with red and blue 3-D glasses or seen a 3-D movie? Red and blue 3-D glasses enable us to see 3-D images even though the images are created in two dimensions. Two very similar images are over-laid but slightly separated. One image is in red and the second image is in blue. Sheets of plastic are then used to make lenses in 3-D glasses, one red and the other blue. This means that the right eye sees the first image, and the left eye sees the slightly different image. The slight difference in perspective, and the fact that each eye can only see one image (both of which look to be the same one), creates an illusion of 3-D.

Elsa's research in nonlinear optics has helped improve the understanding of lasers. These are used in a wide range of applications, including communications and computers. Her research has helped scientists develop ways to better use lasers. She has also studied ways to use lasers and light to improve or replace electronics.

Elsa has written hundreds of papers and won numerous awards. She holds several patents for devices that are used to enhance optical communications, including lasers, waveguides, and detectors.

One of her inventions helps solve a major problem in urban areas. It is a laser device that removes graffiti. The device is portable and designed to remove spray-painted graffiti from a range of surfaces, including stone, brick, and wood. She developed the device when she was the director of laser studies at the University of Southern California.

Ask & Answer

Is there graffiti where you live? Why do you think graffiti is a problem? Can graffiti be considered art?

LASERS AS ART

Lasers are not only powerful scientific tools, they can also be used to create art. Elsa was one of the founders of the company that created the first Laserium light show at the Griffith Observatory. She also helped to develop a mirror and light show for the 1970 World's Fair in Japan. She said of the

Mildred Dresselhaus

Professor Mildred Dresselhaus, who is known as the "queen of carbon," is a professor emeritus of electrical engineering and physics at Massachusetts Institute of Technology. She was Elsa's role model. Elsa says Mildred is "amazing, raised four children, is a concert violinist, has published widely, and doesn't need sleep." Mildred's work related to carbon nanotubes has been cited by thousands of people. It has applications in a wide range of fields, including electrical, biomedical, structural, and environmental engineering.

intense light created by a laser beam, "It's beautiful, incredibly beautiful. It has that sparkling look, and that's magic." Laser light shows are fairly common these days at concerts and outdoor festivals.

> 66 I'm happy to keep doing science and being a mentor to anyone who asks for advice. 99
>
> **—Mildred Dresselhaus**

Mildred is in her 80s. She continues to go to work most days because she loves what she does and is still full of ideas. She was recently the first female to be awarded the Institute of Electrical and Electronics Engineers Medal of Honor.

She says, "Follow your interests, get the best available education and training, set your sights high, be persistent, be flexible, keep your options open, accept help when offered, and be prepared to help others."

CAREER AND TEACHING

Despite being fascinated by the relationship between art and technology, Elsa focused most of her career on research and teaching. She felt she could make a bigger impact in academics than in the art world.

Elsa started her career as a researcher at the California Institute of Technology (CalTech). There, she felt a great deal of frustration with the competitive, male-dominated atmosphere. She felt she constantly had to prove that she was good enough. After several years as a researcher at CalTech, she decided to work in industry for a few years at ITT Telecom Labs.

> **66** The most important thing I've accomplished
> . . . is training young people. They come to me
> and say, 'Do you think we can do this?' I say, 'Try
> it.' And I back 'em up. They need that. **99**
>
> **—Grace Murray Hopper,** computer scientist

In 1981, she returned to academia as a professor at the University of Southern California. She spent more than 20 years as a professor of electrical engineering and director of the Center for Laser Studies at the University of Southern California.

Elsa relocated to Dartmouth College in 1995 to become the dean of the Thayer School of Engineering, another new challenge! Two years as the dean was enough for her, however. After her stint as a dean, she returned to research and teaching at Dartmouth. While she continues to teach two courses at Dartmouth, "Optics" and "Electromagnetic Fields and Waves," retirement is something she's thinking about.

Ask & Answer

What is the relationship between art and technology? Have you ever developed a video game or made pictures out of lights or designed a building using engineering software?

Elsa is one of very few women elected to the National Academy of Engineering, which is a highly prestigious honor. And she was the second female president of the Optical Society of America. Elsa is a fellow of the National Academy of Inventors, the Institute of Electrical and Electronics Engineers, and the Optical Society of America.

Cool Careers:
Special Effects Engineer

Engineers with an interest in optics and computer programming can work behind the scenes to create special effects for movies. While special effects used to be done with smoke and mirrors, most are now created using computers. The role of a special effects engineer is to make fantasies look real. Pixar, the creators of *Monsters, Inc.*, *Brave*, *Inside Out*, *WALL-E*, *Ratatouille*, and lots more movies, hires many engineers to help with special effects. Carla Meninsky, an engineer for Atari who coded the games *Warlords*, *Dodge 'Em*, and *Star Raiders*, says, "I was a bit of an artist, and somewhere along the way had gotten the idea that computers could be used for animation and artists, because in-betweening was so tedious . . . . Of course, everyone thought I was nuts."

Ask & Answer

Are there things you do that make you proud even if no one notices you doing them?

She also belongs to the Society of Women Engineers and the American Physical Society. Other memberships include the National Academy of Engineering and the American Academy of Arts and Sciences.

As a teacher and mentor, Elsa is known for being demanding but patient. Elsa says, "Teaching is so incredibly satisfying and self-justifying." This means that she feels rewarded for doing the work even if no one tells her she is doing a good job. Many of her students have gone on to become professors around the world and to develop their own successful research programs. She says of her students: "I'm creating my own grand-students."

PUBLIC POLICY

Elsa has served as an advisor to government policy-makers for the U.S. Department of Energy, the National Science Foundation, the U.S. Air Force, and other organizations. She has worked hard to help decision-makers and people who make policies understand the technical details associated with their decisions.

One of her roles as an advisor on public policy is to look at and regulate the band of wavelengths available for communications. There is a limited band of available wavelengths that can be used for radio, cell phones, television, satellite communication, and other uses. Governments must work together to share and regulate these resources.

The International Telecommunications Union (ITU), a special branch of the United Nations, is responsible for issues related to information and communication technologies. The United States, along with another 192 countries, are members of the ITU. A committee of representatives from the ITU countries meets regularly, and Elsa has participated in these meetings as a representative of the United States.

LIFE AS A FEMALE SCIENTIST

Elsa has always been full of questions and has never been afraid to ask them. She says, "It is really important for young women to learn to put themselves out there and ask questions if they don't understand something." How will you learn if you don't ask questions? And the chances are good that other students will thank you for asking, since they likely have the same questions.

M. Gertrude Rand (1886-1970)

M. Gertrude Rand was a pioneer in the area of lighting and optics. She was a psychologist who earned a doctoral degree in psychology from Bryn Mawr College in 1911. M. Gertrude was the first woman to receive the Optical Society of America's Edgar D. Tillyer Medal. Her research, much of which she conducted with her husband, Clarence Ferree, focused on how people perceive color as lighting varies.

As a professor of physiological optics at Johns Hopkins University, M. Gertrude helped design the lighting for the Holland Tunnel under the Hudson River. She also helped to establish vision standards for pilots and ship lookouts during World War II. She was the first female fellow of the Illuminating Engineering Society of North America and the recipient of the society's Gold Medal in 1963.

While Elsa notes that discrimination can still be an issue for female scientists, she has not let it get in her way. Once, at a conference, the presenter began his talk with, "Gentlemen . . . ." Noting that she was the only woman in the audience, she called out, "And lady!" Elsa is highly respected in the field of photonics and lasers by men and women alike.

Despite all of her success as a researcher and engineer, Elsa is still surprised by her success and wonders if she just got lucky. This inability to accept success is fairly common, especially among high-achieving women. It is known as the imposter syndrome. Psychologists studying high-achieving people in the 1970s found that those who suffer from this syndrome often feel that their success is because of other factors, such as luck or their relationships.

Stereotype Threat

Stereotype threat is a phenomenon where people feel pressure because they face a task that may confirm a stereotype. Stereotype threat can result in individuals underperforming and in increased levels of stress. Female scientists may feel extra pressure to show that they are good at math and science, a form of stereotype threat.

They feel like a fraud despite evidence that they have worked hard and deserve the success that they have achieved. Elsa recognizes that her feelings are not rational. But she brings it up in an effort to help other female scientists who might face psychological issues, including imposter syndrome and stereotype threat.

FAMILY

Elsa gave birth to the first of her two daughters just a few weeks before defending her doctoral thesis. She proofread her thesis in the maternity ward.

Her original plan was to stay home with the baby. Her mentor and role model had stayed at home to raise her four children and then returned to work, so Elsa decided that is what she would do too. Most women stayed home with their children in those days. But Elsa is not most women. It was clear to her after a couple of months that she would be a better mother if she was working. She decided to return to work.

Elsa and her first husband, also a physicist, researcher, and professor, eventually divorced. But she has been married to her current husband, Bob, for more than 35 years. Bob is an electrical engineer and has been extremely supportive of Elsa's career and family.

Science or Engineering?

Both Elsa and her role model, Mildred Dresselhaus, received degrees in physics but then became professors of engineering. This is not uncommon. Often scientists become engineers and vice versa. Engineering is the application of math and science to create new processes and products. Engineers who work on optics and circuits, such as Elsa and Mildred, need a strong background in physics. Engineers who work on biomedical devices have a strong background in biology. And chemistry is essential for environmental engineering. The line between engineering and applied science is often blurred.

Neither of Elsa's daughters, Lisa and Marla, became an engineer. One earned a PhD in English and the other a degree in communications. But both of them are comfortable with science, math, engineering, and technology, and that has been to their advantage. Lisa and Marla are able to translate technical information and present it to the public. And both have worked for high-tech startup companies. Elsa's daughters are married and live in California.

Lisa suffered from a rare autoimmune disease in her late 20s that resulted in losing her kidneys. She had to go on dialysis and eventually received a kidney transplant with a kidney donated by her husband. Lisa has one daughter, Lila, who is Elsa's oldest granddaughter.

Elsa's other daughter, Marla, has twin daughters, Ashley and Brooke (originally known as baby A and baby B). The twins could not be more different. According to Elsa, one is outgoing and the other is quiet.

Elsa adores all of her grandchildren. She and Bob even bought a home in California so that they could spend more time with their children and grandchildren. Maybe they can nurture a love of engineering in their granddaughters, or at least an appreciation for science, math, and engineering!

Engineering is such an exciting profession, with a huge range of options. Engineers study optics, develop lasers, build new biomedical devices, design special effects, create satellite imaging and communication systems, develop processes to clean up the environment, and so much more. There is something for everyone in engineering!

> 66 Somewhere, something incredible
> is waiting to be known. 99
>
> **—Carl Sagan,**
> astronomer

Timeline

Around 400

- Hypatia becomes head of the Platonist school at Alexandria, Egypt, and teaches math and philosophy.

1794

- The École Polytechnique is started in France to teach military and civil engineering (no women were admitted initially).

1809

- Mary Dixon Kies is the first woman to receive a patent, for a method for weaving straw.

1819

- West Point Military Academy in the United States starts programs in civil and military engineering, modeled on the programs at the École Polytechnique.

1828

- Rensselaer Polytechnic Institute begins teaching civil engineering.

1872

- Emily Warren Roebling takes over the construction oversight of the Brooklyn Bridge after her husband becomes ill. She is credited with completing the bridge.

1873

- Ellen Henrietta Swallow Richards graduates from the Massachusetts Institute of Technology (MIT). She was the first American woman to obtain a degree in chemistry and the first female instructor at MIT. While her degrees were in science, much of her work focused on sanitary engineering.

1894

- Elmina T. Wilson receives a master's degree in civil engineering from Iowa State University. She went on to become the first female civil engineering professor.

1905

- Nora Stanton Blatch Barney receives a degree in civil engineering from Cornell University. She is the first woman to graduate in engineering from Cornell and becomes the first female member of the American Society of Civil Engineers.

Timeline

1906

- Alice Perry graduates from Queen's College in Galway, becoming the first female engineering graduate in Britain.

1912

- Elisa Leonida Zamfirescu is the first female engineer in Europe, graduating from the Royal Academy of Technology in Berlin with a degree in engineering and chemistry.

1920

- Olive Dennis is the second woman to graduate from Cornell University. She becomes a service engineer, the first person to be given that title, for the Baltimore and Ohio Railroad.

1949

- Nancy Fitzroy is the first woman to graduate from Rensselaer Polytechnic Institute with a degree in chemical engineering. She was the first female president of the American Society of Mechanical Engineers.

1952

- The Society of Women Engineers, a national organization based in the United States, is established.

1972

- The École Polytechnique begins to admit women.

1997

- Olin College of Engineering is founded in Massachusetts with the mission of experimenting with innovative engineering education approaches. Of the students graduating in engineering from Olin, 50 percent are women!

2000

- Smith College starts an all-women engineering program. In 2004, the first class of 19 women graduates with a bachelor's degree in engineering.

Timeline

2005

- Limor Fried starts Adafruit Industries, a woman-owned company that sells electronic kits and parts for makers of all ages.

2005

- Ruchi Sanghvi, a computer engineer, is the first female engineer hired by Facebook. She quits working at Facebook in 2011 to start her own company, Cove, which she eventually sells to Dropbox.

2012

- Etsy makes training and hiring female engineers a top priority, increasing their number of female engineers from 3 (out of 47) to 20 (out of 90).

2015

- Naomi Climer becomes the first female president of the Institution of Engineering and Technology.

Ask & Answer

Introduction

- What devices do you wish existed? How would these devices make your life easier and the world a better place?

Chapter 1

- How did early civilizations create technology and systems to meet the needs of community and individuals?
- What will robots of the future do?
- What areas of engineering are you most interested in?

Chapter 2

- What do you do when you realize you've made a mistake?

- Are sports important to you? How do you find a balance between sports and school and other things you love to do?

- How is a robot different from a human? Will robots ever be able to think? Will they ever be able to have emotions?

- Why do new products need to be thoroughly tested in labs before they are used by the general public?

Chapter 3

- Are you and your family prepared for a natural disaster? Where would you go if you had to leave your home? Where would you live?

- Imagine what it would be like to be without access to clean water or housing. How would your life be different?

- Are you good at speaking in front of large groups of people? Will this be an important skill to have in your future?

Chapter 4

- How do your parents' jobs affect your own decisions about what you want to do as an adult?

- Do you have any experience with lasers? What do you know about them?

- Is there graffiti where you live? Why do you think graffiti is a problem? Can graffiti be considered art?

- Are there things you do that make you proud even if no one notices you doing them?

- Lasers and fiber optics have enabled us to communicate and connect with people globally. Do you think we'll ever be able to communicate with other planets? What questions would you ask someone from another planet?

Glossary

3-D printer: a machine or printer that additively creates three-dimensional objects using a range of materials.

activist: someone who pushes for change.

advisor: someone who offers advice and counsel, often in an academic setting.

advocate: recommend or support publically.

agriculture: growing plants and raising animals for food and other products.

algae: a large group of plants that includes seaweed and many types of single-celled plants.

alternative fuels: non-fossil fuels. Alternative fuels include biodiesel, ethanol, vegetable oil, and other fuels produced by natural materials.

anesthesia: the medicine used during an operation to put patients to sleep and keep them from feeling pain.

animation: the process of making still images appear to move.

Archimedes' principle: the idea that when an object is placed in a fluid, it experiences an upward force that is equal to the weight of the fluid that is displaced.

astronomer: a scientist who studies the stars, planets, galaxies, and space.

atom: the smallest particle of matter that cannot be broken down without changing the particle's properties.

atomic clock: a clock that uses an oscillator with a high degree of accuracy.

authentic: genuine or real.

autoimmune disease: a disease that causes the body to attack healthy cells.

autonomous: without human contact.

biology: the science of life and living organisms.

biomechanics: the study of how the human body works.

biomedical engineering: a branch of engineering that combines engineering, biology, and medicine.

bionic eye: an artificial or robotic eye.

buoyancy: the upward force from a fluid that helps an object float.

cardiothoracic: the area of medicine focused on the thorax or chest.

catapult or trebuchet: weapons used to fling heavy objects.

ceramic filter: an inexpensive filter that uses the small pore size of the material (ceramic) to remove unwanted elements.

chemical: a substance that has certain features that can react with other substances.

chemistry: the science of how substances interact, combine, and change.

circuit: a path that lets electricity flow when closed in a loop.

civil engineer: an engineer who designs the built environment such as roads, bridges, and buildings.

coherent: light of the same wavelength.

Glossary

collaborate: to work together with other people.

concave: a surface that curves inward.

conservation: managing and protecting natural resources.

customizable: when something is able to change according to who is using it.

deep space: the space well beyond the earth's atmosphere.

density: the amount of matter in a given space, or mass divided by volume.

developing country: a poor country that is trying to become more advanced.

dexterous: skillful with the hands.

diode: an electronic component.

discrimination: the unjust treatment of people or things that are different.

docked: connected.

drone: a robot that flies.

eccentric: odd, usually in a unique way.

efficacy: the ability to produce an intended result.

electrical charge: a positive or negative imbalance in electricity in a body.

electrical engineer: an engineer who designs systems and processes that use electricity.

electromagnetic: magnetism developed with a current of electricity.

electronics: circuits.

elite: the best of a category of things.

engineer: someone who uses math, science, and creativity to solve problems or meet human needs.

engineering: the use of science and math in the design and construction of things.

enrich: to improve.

entrepreneur: a person who starts and runs a business.

environmental engineer: an engineer who designs systems to protect and improve the environment.

expertise: special skills or knowledge.

environmentally friendly: products and processes that do not harm the environment.

fiber optics: cables made of glass threads that transmit messages using light.

fossil fuels: energy sources such as coal, oil, and natural gas that come from plants and animals that lived millions of year ago.

fraud: a dishonest person or dishonest methods.

frequency: the number of sound waves that pass a specific point each second.

GERD: gastroesophageal reflux disease, a digestive disorder.

Great Depression: a long-term economic crisis that started in 1929.

humble: modest, not proud.

hydrometer: a tool for measuring the density of liquids.

implant: to insert something, usually for medical reasons.

Glossary

imposter syndrome: when people feel like a fraud despite evidence that they have worked hard and deserve the success that they have achieved.

innovate: to come up with a new way of doing something.

integrate: to become part of.

intellectual property: property that comes from the work of the mind.

internship: a training period in service of an employer.

intimidating: making another person fearful with threats or other shows of power.

invasive: spreading rapidly and harmfully.

investor: a person who gives a company money in exchange for future profits.

iteration: the repetition of a process.

laser: light amplification by stimulated emission of radiation. A powerful beam of light.

lasing medium: the substance used in lasers to increase the intensity of the light.

LED: light-emitting diode, which provides very efficient lighting.

lens: an optical device that affects the focus of a light beam.

marketing: communicating in different ways to make a business known.

maser: microwave amplification by stimulated response of radiation.

mass: the amount of material that an object contains.

maternity ward: the area in a hospital that provides care for women during pregnancy and childbirth.

mechanical engineer: an engineer who designs mechanical devices and processes such as machines and cars.

metallurgy: the study of metals.

microwave radiation: radiation with wavelengths that are 1 meter to 1 millimeter in length.

minimally invasive surgery: surgery that reduces the number of cuts and trauma to the body.

nanotechnology: the study and development of products and processes at a *really* small scale.

NGO: a nongovernmental organization that is nonprofit and set up by ordinary people, usually to help people or the environment.

Nobel Prize: an international prize awarded for outstanding contributions in science, literature, economics, and the promotion of peace.

nonlinear optics: the study of how intense light is able to change the material through which it travels and the light itself.

open source: resources that are accessible and modifiable by anyone.

optical illusion: an image that is misleading or may be viewed multiple different ways.

optics: the study of the properties and behavior of light.

Glossary

oscillator (electronic): an electronic circuit that produces a regular signal.

patent: legal protection for a new idea.

photon: a small particle of light.

photovoltaic: a device that produces electricity when exposed to sunlight.

physical therapy: the treatment of injury or disease through physical methods.

physics: the science of matter and energy.

pitch: a short presentation aimed at convincing someone that you have an idea that could be successful.

policy: a system of principles used to guide decisions.

process: an activity that takes several steps to complete.

product: an item, such as a book or clothing, that is made and sold to people.

prototype: a working model or mock-up that allows engineers to test their solution.

psychology: the study of the mind and how humans behave.

purify: remove unwanted particles.

radio telescope: an instrument used to detect radio-frequency radiation.

research: a systematic study.

robot: a machine that moves and performs different functions that are controlled through circuits and computer programs.

rover: an automated vehicle or robot.

rotational motion: movement around the center of something.

satellite: a manmade object that is placed in orbit.

sewage: waste products.

simulation: the appearance or effect of something that is used for practice.

slide rule: a mechanical device used to solve math problems.

social good: an action that benefits a large number of people.

social robot: a robot that is capable of interacting with humans.

solar energy: energy from the sun.

soliton: a self-reinforcing solitary wave.

startup: a new company that is trying to market a new product or process.

stereotype threat: a phenomenon where people feel pressure because they face a task that may confirm a stereotype.

sustainability: living in a way that uses resources wisely, so they don't run out.

toxic: poisonous.

ultrasound: sound waves with a very high frequency.

United Nations: an international organization created to promote peace and cooperation among nations.

usability: how easy and relevant an object or process is to use.

wavelength: the distance from the high point of one wave to the high point of the next wave.

Resources

Books

- *Girls Think of Everything: Stories of Ingenious Inventions by Women.* Catherine Thimmesh. HMH Books for Young Readers, 2002.

- *Setting the Record Straight: The History and Evolution of Women's Professional Achievement in Engineering.* Betty Reynolds and Jill Tietjen. White Apple Press, 2001.

- *Annie Sullivan and the Trials of Helen Keller.* Joseph Lambert. Disney-Hyperion, 2012.

- *The New Way Things Work.* David Macaulay. HMH, 1998.

- *The Art of Tinkering.* Karen Wilkinson and Mike Petrich. Weldon Owen, 2014.

- *Gizmos & Gadgets: Creating Science Contraptions that Work (& Knowing Why).* Jill Frankel Hauser. Williamson Publishing, 1999.

- *Gourmet Lab: The Scientific Principles Behind Your Favorite Foods.* Sarah Reeves Young. National Science Teachers Association Press, 2011.

- *Make Your Own Musical Instruments.* Anna-Marie D'Cruz. PowerKids Press, 2009.

- *Making Things Move: DIY Mechanisms for Inventors, Hobbyists, and Artists.* Dustyn Roberts. McGraw-Hill Education, 2010.

- *Music and Mathematics: From Pythagoras to Fractals.* Edited by John Fauvel, Raymond Flood, and Robin Wilson. Oxford University Press, 2006.

- *Spinning.* Sara E. Hoffmann. Lerner Classroom, 2012.

- *The Art of Construction: Projects and Principles for Beginning Engineers & Architects.* Mario Salvadori. Chicago Review Press, 2000.

Resources

Websites

- Engineer Girl website: *engineergirl.org*
- Engineering, Go For it!: *egfi-k12.org/about/*
- American Society of Engineering Education: *asee.org*
- LuminAID Lab: *luminaid.com*
- Optics 4 Kids: *optics4kids.org/home*
- The Society of Women Engineers: *societyofwomenengineers.swe.org*
- About Chemistry: *chemistry.about.com/od/letsmakeslime/tp/slimerecipes.htm*
- Chem4Kids: *chem4kids.com*
- Engineering Encounters - Bridge Design Contest: *bridgecontest.org*
- How Stuff Works - Gear Ratios: *science.howstuffworks.com/transport/engines-equipment/gear-ratio.htm*
- PBS Building Big: *pbs.org/wgbh/buildingbig/bridge*
- PBS Nova: *pbs.org/wgbh/nova/physics/galileo-experiments.html*
- PBS Parents: *pbs.org/parents/crafts-for-kids/super-bouncy-balls*
- PhET Interactive Simulations: *phet.colorado.edu/en/simulation/density*
- Squishy Circuits: *courseweb.stthomas.edu/apthomas/SquishyCircuits*
- How Things Fly: *howthingsfly.si.edu/gravity-air/buoyancy*
- TED-ED: Archimedes' Principle: *ed.ted.com/lessons/mark-salata-how-taking-a-bath-led-to-archimedes-principle*

QR Code Glossary

- Page 5: kidsactivitiesblog. com/55055/15-easy-catapults-to-make
- Page 6: youtube.com/ watch?v = y0SnFCs9z1g
- Page 6: youtube.com/ watch?v = KMNwXUCXLdk
- Page 15: youtube.com/ watch?feature = player_embedded&v = ogBX18maUiM
- Page 15: braingate2.org
- Page 16: engineergirl.org
- Page 20: technologyreview. com/featuredstory/528141/ the-thought-experiment
- Page 25: cyphyworks.com/about
- Page 25: irobot.com
- Page 30: seas.harvard.edu/ news/2010/10/undergrads-design-sweet-catapults
- Page 33: jibo.com
- Page 35: intuitivesurgical. com/products/davinci_surgical_system/davinci_surgical_system_si
- Page 37: nasdaq.com/ press-release/intuitive-surgical-and-trumpf-medical-team-up-to-address-hospitals-need-for-operating-room-20151014-00054
- Page 38: nature.com/news/ the-printed-organs-coming-to-a-body-near-you-1.17320
- Page 38: the3doodler.com
- Page 48: luminaid.com
- Page 50: en.wikipedia.org/ wiki/A_Long_Walk_to_Water
- Page 56: store.sundancesolar. com/sunbender-do-it-yourself-solar-led-jar-light-kit-pre-wired-no-soldering
- Page 56: instructables.com/ id/Best-Solar-Oven
- Page 59: ted.com/talks/ amy_smith_shares_simple_lifesaving_design?language = er
- Page 62: 300house.com
- Page 67: adafruit.com
- Page 67: adainitiative. org/2013/01/15/limor-ladyada-fried-entrepreneur-of-2012
- Page 71: loc.gov/resource/ magbell.12400313/?st = gallery
- Page 76: optics4kids.org/ home/content/illusions
- Page 84: patrickmccray. com/2014/12/26/art-at-the-speed-of-light/?utm_content = bufferda7ce&utm_medium = social&utm_source = twitter. com&utm_campaign = buffer

Index

Index